I Can't Carry That In My Backpack!

By Wanda B. & Latanya E. Nichols

Illustrated by
Joseph Lonnell Jones

Published By:

ISBN-978-1466330719

This is dedicated to my three wonderful children: Alenda, Jauquisha , and Dankerie. Also, to my beautiful grand-daughter Joy "Jade" Butler.

Wanda B.

This book is dedicated to my wonderful family who has supported me throughout the years as I have worked to accomplish personal and professional goals. Love you Willie, Desirae, Wilicia, Diongelia, and Tommy. Also, to my beautiful grandchildren Tenauri, DeLani, and Tawny, the next generation, with love...

L.E. Nichols

A very special dedication and appreciation goes to Lonnie!! We thank God for you! You made this book come to life. There are no words to express how truly grateful we are. Thank you!

L.E Nichols & Wanda B.

I want to Thank You Wanda and Latanya for this opportunity and your PATIENCE while I held my "Day" job to illustrate your book. I also want to thank my Wife and Daughters for having so much patience with me. It wasn't easy for you all to sit idly by while I dived into my sketch pad and computer after a hard day of work. I only hope to one day be able to repay you all (with more un-fatigued TIME) for your undying love for me.

Lonnie J.

"The good of a book lies in its being read. A book is made up of signs that speak of other signs, which in their turn speak of things."

— Umberto Eco, The Name of the Rose

"Change happens when we seek to be the difference."

-Anonymous

Darren

Darren was asleep, but awakened in a panicked fright,
only to hear his parents arguing again, in the middle of the night.
They were screaming and shouting at one another,
so he jumped out of bed and tried to calm his father and mother.

His mother insisted that Darren go back to bed.
He said, "no! I'm going to get you a band-aid instead."
He placed bandages on her face, arms, hands, and feet.
She thanked him for his help but insisted that he get some sleep.
He was heartbroken, angry, and filled with rage.
Like a wild lion trapped and locked in a cage.

Darren tried to sleep like his mother said.
But, he had so many thoughts going through his head.
He was scared for his mother but didn't know what to do.
His father was abusive and would beat him, too.
Darren jumped up and put a chair against the door.
Then grabbed his blankets and made a pallet on the floor.

He lay quiet as he released his own tears.
Thinking about the mistreatment his mother took over the years.
His parents argued every single day.
He wondered why his mother chose to stay.
They fought about everything; from this to that.
Anger weighed heavy in his backpack.

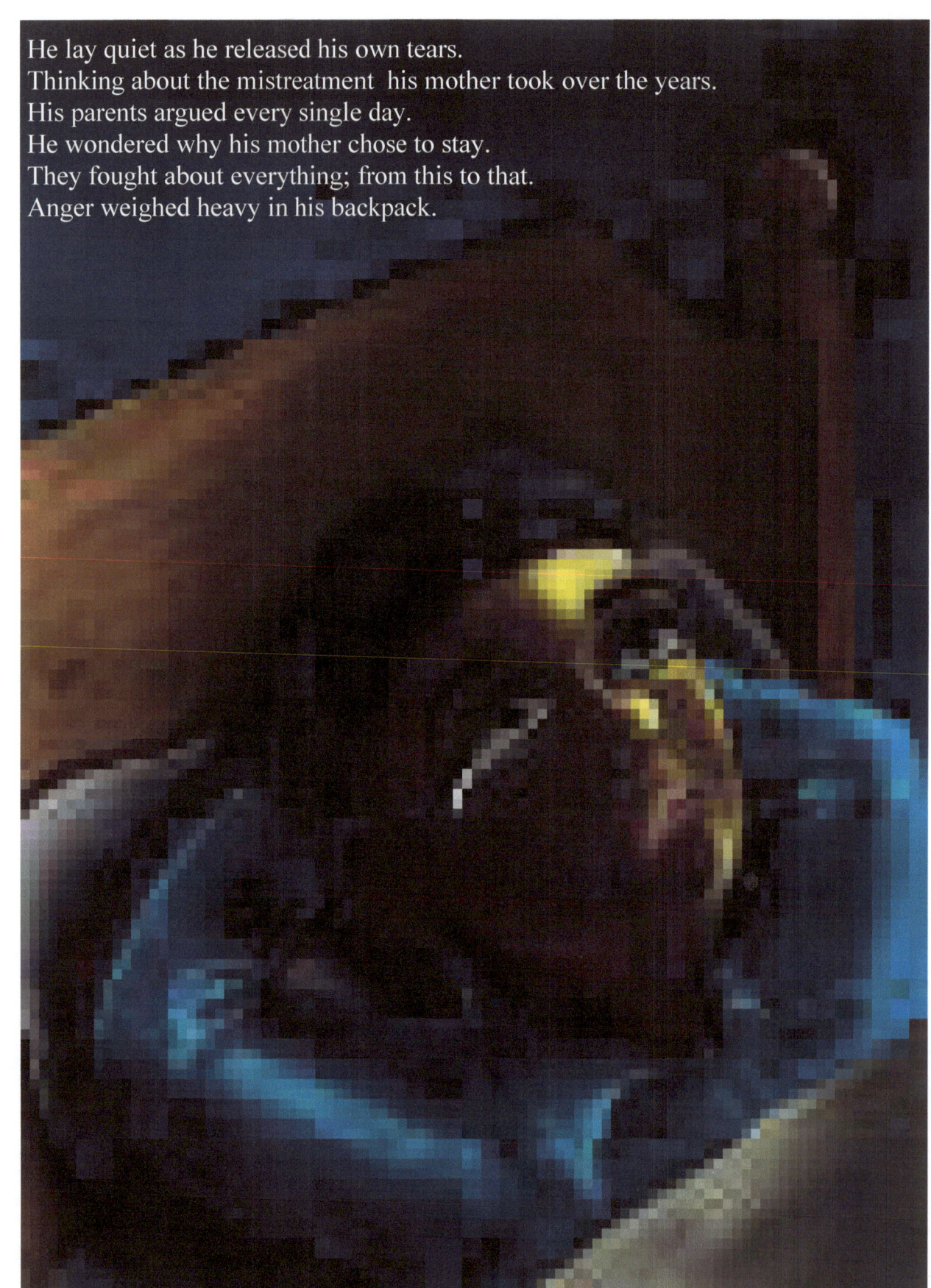

He carried this misery to school, trying to hide it under his desk.
On one particular day, he failed his language arts test.

Darren couldn't concentrate on his work in class.
"Is something wrong?" his science teacher asked.
How could he explain what his father had done?
Were there others like him, or was he the only one?

Sorrowfully, he told his teacher about the fight.
She explained to him that hitting wasn't right.
His teacher let him know that he wasn't alone.
She said, "Many children live in an abusive home."
Then she said, "Children can't choose who their parents are.
But, they can report abuse before it goes too far."

After school, Darren ran home as fast as he could.
He was hoping his father had left for good.
He was disappointed when he saw his father at home.
His mother wasn't there. She was gone.
Darren's heart broke and filled with grim.
He wondered if she would come back for him.

Darren didn't want to stay there alone with his dad.
So he went to his room and packed everything he had.
Two hours had passed and his mother still wasn't home.
He wondered what could be taking her so long.

Darren jumped to his feet as he heard footsteps draw near.
The jingle at the doorknob filled his heart with fear.
He inhaled a deep breath and stayed as quiet as a mouse,
His mother entered and said, "We're moving to grandma's house."

"If you only have one smile in you, give it to the people you love."
-Maya Angelou

Reflective Change Activity

Use this page to reflect on Darren's situation. How might his circumstances at home have an effect on other areas of his life? Think about how you would respond to support Darren. What would it look and sound like?

Charles

"I can't wait to get to school," Charles said to himself, as he searched in the darkness to find his clothes. He remembered putting them on the dresser just before the sun went down last night. Never mind, he thought. I'll never find them. I'll just have to put on the pants and shirt I wore yesterday. No one will ever know. "Now, all I have to do is find my sneakers," he grunted slightly frustrated. He only owned one pair. It was one of the many problems he carried in his backpack.

Charles thought about many things as he and his brothers walked to school. Being the eldest of his three boys kept him very busy. His mother worked two jobs and they hardly saw her during the week, and much less on the weekends. However, Charles loved his brothers and he knew his mother loved them. Responsibility was something else he put in his backpack.

Charles and his brothers went directly to the cafeteria. He could smell the eggs and sausages. Mmm, I can't wait for something hot to eat, he thought as they stood in line. He was so anxious to eat that he didn't notice the other kids making fun of him and his brothers. Their clothes were wrinkled and a little dirty. Even though he was embarrassed, Charles knew that getting a hot breakfast was worth putting his shame in his backpack.

Ms. Wilder noticed that Charles was doing his math assignment in her class. She saw how sad he looked and knew something was wrong. She allowed him to continue with his math assignment. After class, Ms. Wilder asked Charles to remain seated and then sat in the desk next to him. "What's wrong, Charles?" She asked. "You look so sad," she added, softly.

"I have a lot of things going on, Ms. Wilder," Charles answered. "Is there anything I can do?" Ms. Wilder asked. "No, Ma'am." Charles dropped his head. "My mom works two jobs and we don't have any power at home. I have much to do before it gets dark." He stood up. "I really have to go." He put his heartache inside his backpack.

By lunchtime, Charles had homework assignments from his math and science classes. He wondered why he needed to learn math and science. He thought, I'm never going to use this stuff anyway! Then he worried about not being able to complete his homework before nightfall. Having no electricity made his days difficult. He had to make sure his brothers were fed and bathe before bedtime. He sighed as he stood in the lunch line waiting for his last hot meal of the day. He ate his lunch, but saved his apple and juice to share with his brothers.

Charles mind raced ahead of him as he and his brothers walked home. He hoped his mother was able to pay the electric bill. He thought about all the homework he had yet to do. He thought about what they were going to wear the next day. Their clothes were dirty and in need of laundry. He thought about what he was going to feed his brothers; peanut butter and jelly or maybe tuna from the can. The more he worried, the heavier his backpack felt.

Charles wanted to make the best of the situation. He came up with a great idea to get clothes washed and have fun at the same time. It was a very hot day. His brothers could wash, play, and bathe all at the same time. He said, "Hey guys! Let's play waterfall wash."

"Easy!" Charles blurted excited.
 "First you have to go look in the laundry basket and find two pair of pants, two shirts, and two pair of socks. Oh! And, grab two pair of underwear."

They ran inside the house and gathered their clothes. "What do we do with them now?" asked Bobby.

Charles said, "I'm going to go in the back yard and fill up the old wash-bin with water and laundry soap. You two have to do your homework while I wash the clothes. When I'm done, you have to come out and put on a shirt and a pair of pants, then run under the waterfall until all the soap is rinsed from your clothes." "Remember to put on your swimming shorts," Charles added.

27

"What happens after all the soap is rinsed out of them?" asked Bobby, yelling out the kitchen window. "You have to take them off and hang them on the fence so they can dry, said Charles" "That sounds like fun," said Raymond, the middle brother, as they watched Charles fill the wash-bin with water. "The first one to rinse and hang up all their clothes is the winner," Charles concluded.

Charles made sure his brothers were done with their homework before he called them out to start the game. He decided to join them for a few minutes of fun. Charles smiled as he watched them run and play underneath his homemade waterfall. The cold water didn't bother them at all on the warm sunny day. They were having fun. And, for that moment, Charles had forgotten the worries still weighing heavy in his backpack.

As his brothers continued to play waterfall, Charles managed to fix them peanut butter and jelly sandwiches, read chapter three of his language practice book, and complete the rest of his math homework.

Charles felt good knowing that they had clean clothes for the next day and no one would tease him or his brothers at school.

Charles' backpack felt a lot lighter when he picked it up.
Charles was surprised to see his mother come home just as he put his
brothers to bed. "Mom, you're home!" Charles said, happily.
"Yes son, my boss gave me the rest of the night off. And, I got a promotion
with a higher salary!"

The boys jumped out of bed to welcome their mother. They told her about the waterfall game. She laughed with tears of joy then tucked them all in bed. She read them a bedtime story by candlelight. She promised them that she had a big surprise for them tomorrow.

Charles got up early the next morning and prepared his brothers clothes. He and his brothers dressed quickly then hurried off to school.

Charles smiled as he reached in his backpack and found a note his mother had written. It read: Thanks for all of your hard work son. I put a little surprise in your math book, love mom.

He reached in his backpack and pulled out his math book and was overjoyed to see a five dollar bill between the pages.

Ms. Wilder could see that something had changed. She said, "Charles, you look very happy today." "I am! I am," he said.

"My mom is taking care of that matter we discussed earlier in the week." "She said she had a surprise for me and my brothers when we get home from school." "From the smile on your face, I think it's going to be a good surprise," said Ms. Wilder. Charles let out a burly laugh. "I think so too, Ms. Wilder."

Charles and his brothers hurried home. He felt as though everything was going to be okay. When he and his brothers arrived home, the power was back on and their mother had cooked them a hearty, wholesome meal. After dinner, Charles and his mother emptied his backpack of worries, shame, and heartache.

Reflective Change Activity

Use this page to reflect on Charles and his situation. How might his circumstances at home have an effect on other areas of his life? Think about how you would respond to support Charles. What would it look and sound like?

"The highest form of wisdom is kindness."
-The Talmud

The smartest kid in school wasn't smart at all,
he was a bully named Dominic Hall.

Dominic bullied everyone no matter their height,
being trained in Karate, he knew how to fight.

None of the students called him out of his name,
even though his hair grew wild like a lion's mane.

He was different, gifted some would say,
but the good side of him, he choose not to display.
No one understood why he was such a mean kid,
they couldn't figure out why he did the things he did.
He blew spitballs at students, on the ceiling, and the floor,
he even spit a bunch on the classroom door.

Everyone wondered if he acted the same way at home,
but they felt it best that Dominic be left alone.
In class there was tension in the air,
and students glared at him, but he didn't care.

Whenever the teacher chose someone else to answer a question,
Dominic became so angry that he voiced his objection.
At times, he punched anyone who would raise their hand,
Then he'd bang on his desk like a drummer in a band.
His teacher reminded him to keep his hands and feet to himself
but he was defiant and decided to behave with mischief.
He disobeyed her by yelling out and then jumping to his feet.
Dominic jumped up high and landed on his seat.

"I don't have to listen to you," Dominic screamed with a mighty roar,
the teacher said, "Dominic, I won't tolerate your inappropriate behavior
anymore." She didn't bother to write him a referral or give him a pass,
she called for the Dean to come and watch over her class.

She walked Dominic to Principal Watson's office as fast as she could,
he laughed on the way because he thought it would do no good.

He believed his parents didn't care about anything he did,
and sometimes he hated being the only kid.
His nanny, tutor, and trainer he saw everyday,
he felt he could get attention another way.
As the day went by, he pulled and tugged at his hair,
convincing himself that his parents didn't care.

The principal called every number listed in Dominic's file,
leaving message after message, but knew it would take a while.
The principal found something constructive for Dominic to brew,
writing an apology letter to the teacher and class was due.
He called Dominic's parents again as the day went by,
refusing to give up on them, he gave it one last try.

At the principal's optimism and to Dominic's surprise,
his parents showed up with disappointment in their eyes.

Dominic's father let him know that he was not happy at all,
and disappointed because the principal had to call.
His choice to be a bully and disrespectful was wrong in every way,
but Dominic's father promised that tomorrow would be a better day.

On the way home, Dominic started feeling bad inside,
his parents talked to him about bullying, during the entire ride.
Dominic's father admitted that he should've paid him more attention,
and being disrespectful was the other thing he needed to mention.
Dominic cried when his father shared with him a very true fact,
it was wrong of him to carry the need for attention in his backpack.
Dominic got his father's attention unlike ever before,
and promised not to be disrespectful or a bully anymore.

His eyes widened because apologizing was something new,
He apologized to his teacher and classmates, too.

Dominic promised he wouldn't be disrespectful or blow spitballs anymore,
his classmates liked his new look which encouraged Dominic evermore.

Reflective Change Activity

Use this page to reflect on Dominic's situation. How might his circumstances at home have an effect on other areas of his life? Think about how you would respond to support Dominic. What would it look and sound like?

Only the beginning of the end vignettes

I Can't Carry That In My Backpack!

Latanya Nichols has been married for twenty years and is a mother of three. She earned

her Masters Degree in Elementary Education, and is certified in Educational Leadership by the Florida Department of Education. She is a lifelong learner currently completing a doctoral degree in leadership and higher education. She lives in Orlando, Florida, with her husband, three daughters and grandchildren. Although this is her first book within a series, she has written grants for service learning projects, professional staff development, and 21st Century after school programs.

Lonnell Jones is a married father of three girls and one grandson. He is a proud member

of Laborers Local 1058 in Pittsburgh, PA where he is certified as a Traffic Control Specialist for construction projects for heavy highway construction. Graphic art is his first love. He received his formal training by God and is certified by the Art Institute of Pittsburgh; graduating in 1997 as an Animator, skilled in 2D/3D animation techniques. He worked as an Animator and Character Designer for KO Interactive in Pittsburgh until the company relocated. He aided in the building of theater sets for the Kuntu Reporatory Theater on the campus of the University of Pittsburgh, for Founding Director Dr. Vernel Lillie.

Wanda Butler a single mother of three is well experienced in life altering challenges. She

has battled abuse, addiction, and homelessness. Presently she is acquiring her Bachelors in Psychology with the goal of achieving her Masters in Education; and thereafter, a Doctoral degree. Her focus of study will encircle psychosocial behavior therapy and rehabilitation. She plans to use her experience and education to be a motivational speaker. She speaks monthly at the CFDFL (Center for Drug Free Living) and is a member of GMWA (Gospel Music Workshop of America). She has served as a volunteer cheerleading coach for the Orlando Junior Predators for seven years under the direction of her God-sister Tonjali Frost. Wanda re-discovered her passion for writing and realized the need for children to have stories that are relevant to real life situations.

The diversity in "I Can't Carry That in My Backpack" series provides stimulating classroom, professional development, and literary circle discussions. The vignettes within each series provide thought-provoking and debatable subjects that are intended to broaden the teacher and students' outlook and perception while encouraging collaborative exchanges and thoughts.
These educational and inspirational series will cultivate motivation, individuality, group interaction, collaboration, and leadership.

Series I   Elementary
Series II   Middle School
Series III   High School

For ordering, please contact: Latanya E. Nichols: latanyanichols@yahoo.com
Progressive Professionalism at 6500 Arundel Drive, Orlando, Florida 32818
 or P.O. Box 585353 Orlando, Fl. 32858-5353

For graphic artist, please contact: Joseph Lonnell Jones: Lonnie3d1@hotmail.com